Health Facts

All About
Digestion

D1297832

Donna Bailey

STECK-VAUGHN
LIBRARY
A Division of Steck-Vaughn Company

Austin, Texas

How to Use This Book

This book tells you many things about how you digest your food. There is a Table of Contents on the next page. It shows you what each double page of the book is about. For example, pages 10 and 11 tell you about "Food and the Body."

On many of these pages you will find some words that are printed in **bold** type. The bold type shows you that these words are in the Glossary on pages 46 and 47. The Glossary explains the meaning of some words that may be new to you.

At the very end of the book there is an Index. The Index tells you where to find certain words in the book. For example, you can use it to look up words like esophagus, small intestine, carbohydrates, gall bladder, and other words to do with your food and digestion.

© Copyright 1991, text, Steck-Vaughn Company

All rights reserved. No reproduction, copy, or transmission of this publication may be made without written permission.

Printed and bound in the United States of America
1 2 3 4 5 6 7 8 9 0 LB 95 94 93 92

Library of Congress Cataloging-In-Publication Data

Bailey, Donna.
    All about digestion / Donna Bailey.
        p.   cm. — (Health facts)
    Includes index.
    Summary: Discusses the process of digestion, the parts of the digestive system that make it possible, and related topics such as food and its importance to good health.
        ISBN 0-8114-2781-1
        1. Digestion—Juvenile literature. 2. Gastrointestinal system—Juvenile literature. [1. Digestion. 2. Digestive system. 3. Nutrition.] I. Title. II. Series: Bailey, Donna. Health facts.
    QP145.B25   1990   90-41010
    612.3—dc20   CIP AC

Contents

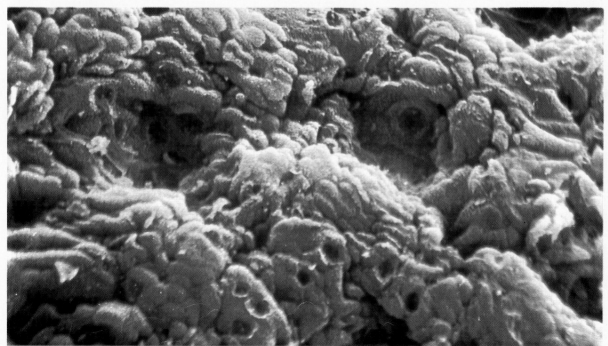

Introduction

All living creatures need food to stay alive. Food gives us **energy** to move, to think, to work, and to play.

Energy from the Sun in the form of heat and light makes plants grow, like the wheat in this field shown in the picture below.

Energy is stored in food. Animals get energy by eating plants or by eating animals that eat plants.

The picture shows a **food chain** in the sea. Plants are usually at the bottom of any food chain. Tiny plants and creatures that drift in the sea are eaten by larger creatures and small fish. These fish in turn are eaten by much larger fish. These larger fish may be caught and eaten by seabirds, by animals, or by humans.

people in different parts of the world enjoy different kinds of food

Hunters and Farmers

Thousands of years ago, people moved from place to place looking for plants to eat, and hunting wild animals for food.

The first farmers lived in the river valleys of the Middle East and Egypt. They began to sow seeds and grow crops for food.

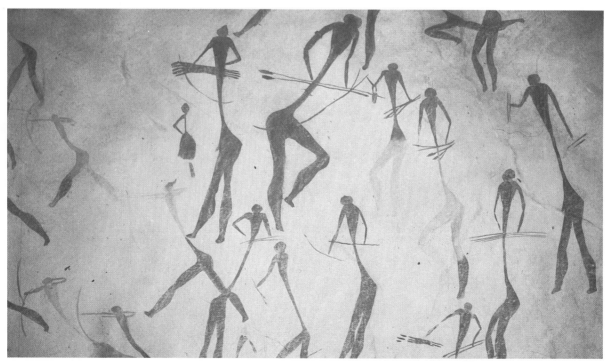

Thousands of years later, in the 1700s and 1800s, engineers invented many different machines, like the one in the picture. Farmers could now grow more crops and harvest them more quickly. The farmers sent their extra crops to feed the people living in the cities.

Today not so many people grow crops or raise animals for their own food. Most people go to a store to buy food. We can buy all sorts of food from many different countries.

Food Today

The picture shows workers picking pineapples and putting them on a conveyor belt, which carries the fruit to where they will be packed in boxes and sent overseas.

picking pineapples in Hawaii

food in this supermarket comes from many countries

Once a crop has been picked, it does not stay fresh for long. **Bacteria** start working to break down the food, so it soon goes bad. Drying, salting, freezing, and pickling food can stop the bacteria from working.

Keeping food cold slows down the rate at which bacteria can work. **Irradiation** is another way of keeping food fresh. This new process is still being tested to make sure it is safe to use on food.

Today many people eat food that has been prepared or pre-cooked before it is deep frozen.

food in a fridge or freezer keeps fresh much longer

9

Food and the Body

When you run and play, you use up a lot of energy. You need food to replace the energy that you have used.

When you eat some food, it has to be broken down so that the **nutrients** in the food can pass into your blood. First, you bite off some food, such as a slice of melon, and chew it well to mix it with the **saliva** in your mouth.

Then you swallow the food and **muscles** push it down your **esophagus** into your stomach. **Enzymes** in the stomach break down the food into small pieces, before the partly-digested food moves into your **small intestine.** Nutrients then pass into the blood, and are used up or are stored in the **liver.**

The waste material goes into the **large intestine** and extra water is taken out. Solid waste is passed out through the **rectum.**

The Digestive System

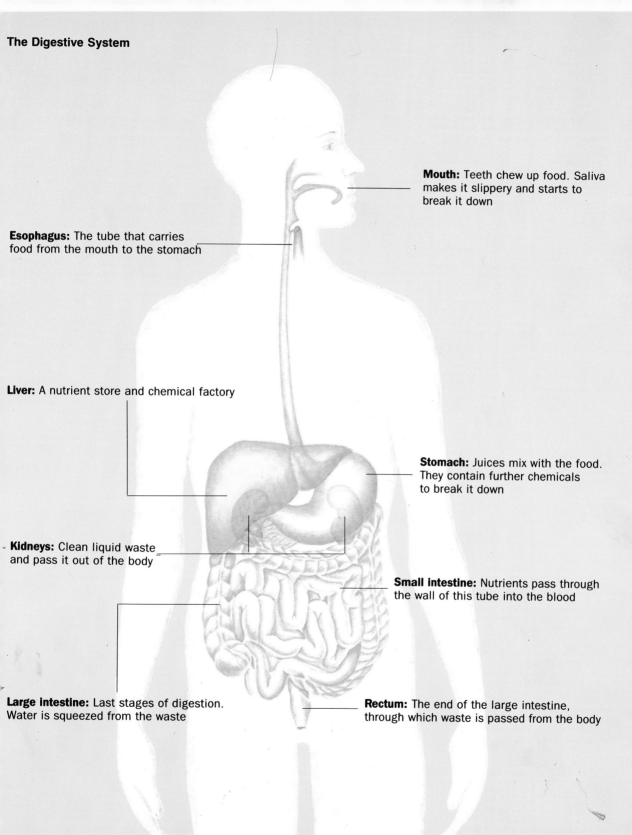

Mouth: Teeth chew up food. Saliva makes it slippery and starts to break it down

Esophagus: The tube that carries food from the mouth to the stomach

Liver: A nutrient store and chemical factory

Stomach: Juices mix with the food. They contain further chemicals to break it down

Kidneys: Clean liquid waste and pass it out of the body

Small intestine: Nutrients pass through the wall of this tube into the blood

Large intestine: Last stages of digestion. Water is squeezed from the waste

Rectum: The end of the large intestine, through which waste is passed from the body

What Is Food Made Of?

Food contains different nutrients. A **carbohydrate** called starch in bread, cereals, rice, and potatoes keeps us warm and gives us energy. Sugar is a carbohydrate, too, but it has hardly any other nutrients. Starch and sugar break down in the body and make **glucose.**

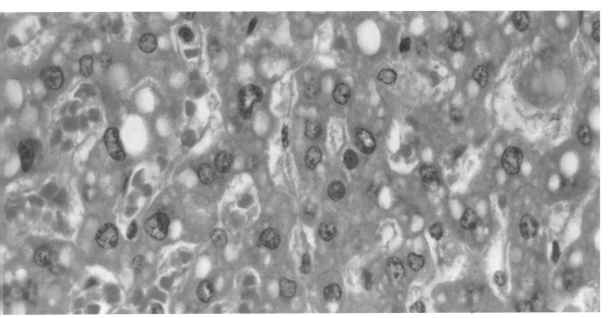

Fats broken down inside the body pass into the blood to give us energy. The photo, taken under a **microscope,** shows drops of fat inside the liver. Extra fat is stored as a layer of fat on your body.

Proteins, found in meat, fish, cheese, and eggs, are needed to build new **cells.** We cannot store extra protein, so any protein that is not needed is passed out in our **urine.**

fish gives us protein to help the body grow

Food at Work

Dietary fiber, found in green, leafy vegetables, grain, and the skins of fruit helps us digest the rest of the food we eat.

Vitamins and **minerals** in the food we eat are also important to help keep our bodies healthy.

sunshine makes your body produce vitamin D

Vitamins help release the energy from carbohydrates, fats, and proteins. The chart shows all the different vitamins and some of the foods they are found in. Each vitamin does a different job and helps a different part of the body.

Vitamin	... found in	good for ...
A	dairy products vegetables fruit	skin, ears, nose, throat, eyes
B₁ thiamine	cereals bread dried beans	digestion, carbohydrate control
B₂ riboflavin	poultry dairy products meat	skin, oxygen for cells
Niacin	meat fish dried beans bread, cereals	nervous and digestive system
Vitamin C	citrus fruit green vegetables tomatoes	teeth and gums, action of minerals
Vitamin D	milk dairy products fish cod-liver oil	bones and teeth, controls calcium and phosphorus
Vitamin E	vegetable oil grains meat, especially liver	cell tissues
Vitamin K	vegetables grains	blood clotting

Biting and Chewing

You use your teeth to bite and chew food such as this sandwich.

You should always make sure that you brush your teeth carefully after each meal so that they stay clean and healthy.

brushing your teeth removes the scraps of food that can cause decay

The sharp, square teeth at the front, the incisors, are used for cutting and biting. The pointed canines are used for tearing food, and the big flat teeth farther back, the molars and premolars, grind the food into a smooth mixture.

Each tooth is covered by hard white **enamel,** and beneath the enamel is a layer of yellow bone-like **dentine.** The soft pulp in the middle contains the **blood vessels** and **nerve fibers.**

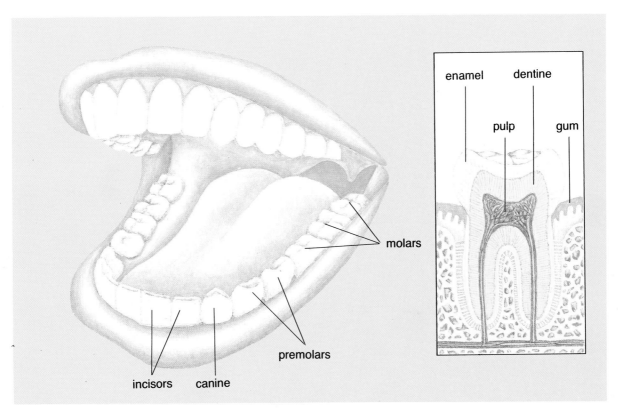

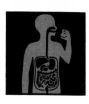

Swallowing Food

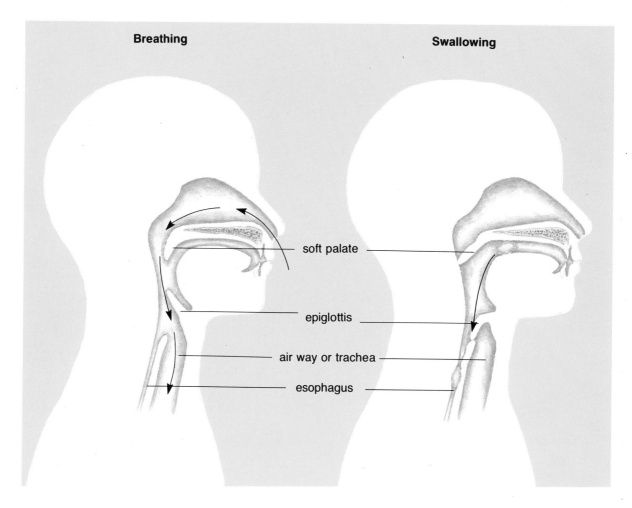

Breathing

Swallowing

soft palate

epiglottis

air way or trachea

esophagus

When you swallow food, the **soft palate** and the **epiglottis** block off the airway or **trachea** to stop food from going down into your **lungs.** If food does go down the wrong tube, it will make you choke.

After the food has gone into your stomach, the **sphincter** muscle at the bottom of the esophagus stops any food from being squeezed back up again.

The stomach wall stretches to hold all the food, and the strong stomach muscles squeeze to churn up the food. In the stomach the food mixes with gastric juices which help break it down. A **mucus** lining protects the stomach wall from these gastric juices.

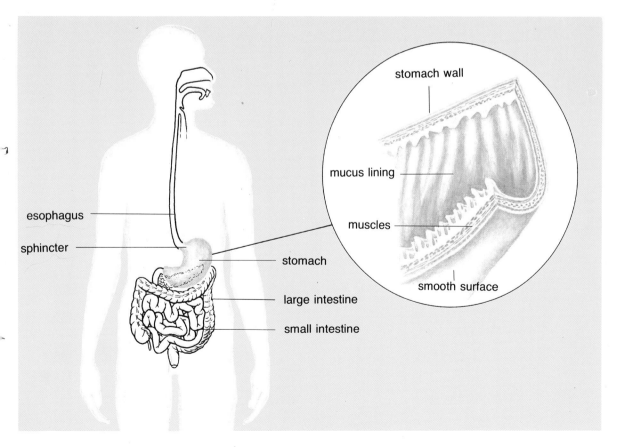

esophagus

sphincter

stomach

large intestine

small intestine

stomach wall

mucus lining

muscles

smooth surface

Into the Blood

After food leaves the stomach, it moves into the **duodenum.** In the duodenum, juices from the **pancreas** and **gall bladder** break down the food even more.

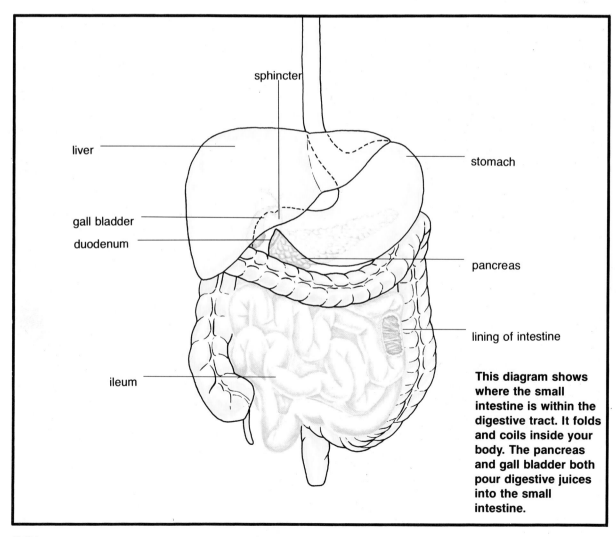

liver

sphincter

stomach

gall bladder

duodenum

pancreas

lining of intestine

ileum

This diagram shows where the small intestine is within the digestive tract. It folds and coils inside your body. The pancreas and gall bladder both pour digestive juices into the small intestine.

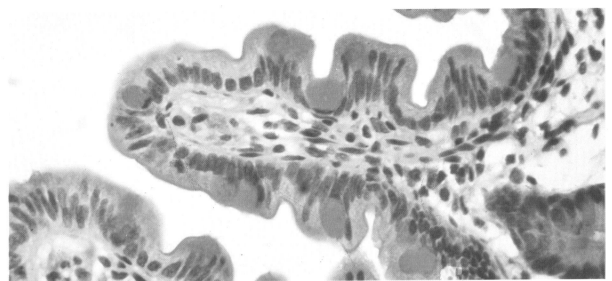

villi take in nutrients

Bile from the gall bladder breaks up the large drops of fat into smaller droplets so that they can be taken in by the body.

The partly-digested food then passes from the duodenum to the **ileum.** Inside the small intestine, are millions of tiny **villi.** Nutrients pass from the digested food to the blood vessels inside the villi. In addition to the blood vessels, each villus has tiny tubes which take in some of the digested fats.

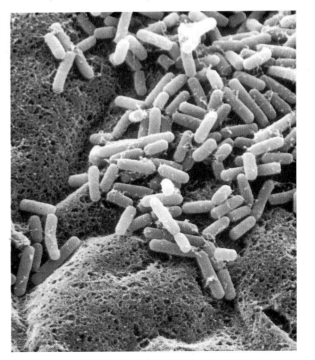

bile breaking down fat

21

The Liver

The athletes in the picture use lots of energy to help them run fast. The energy comes from the glucose in their bodies.

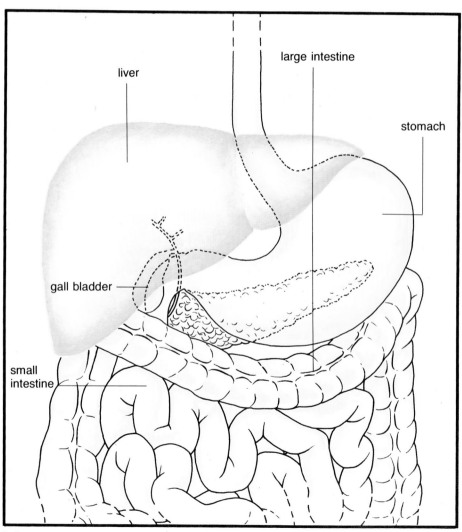

liver

large intestine

stomach

gall bladder

small intestine

The portal vein carries blood full of nutrients from the small intestine. Glucose is stored as **glycogen** inside the six-sided cells of the liver. When it is needed, the glucose is carried in the bloodstream away from the liver along the hepatic vein, and then to every cell in the body.

The hepatic artery carries blood from the **heart** to the liver.

The bile duct carries bile, which is made in the liver, to the gall bladder.

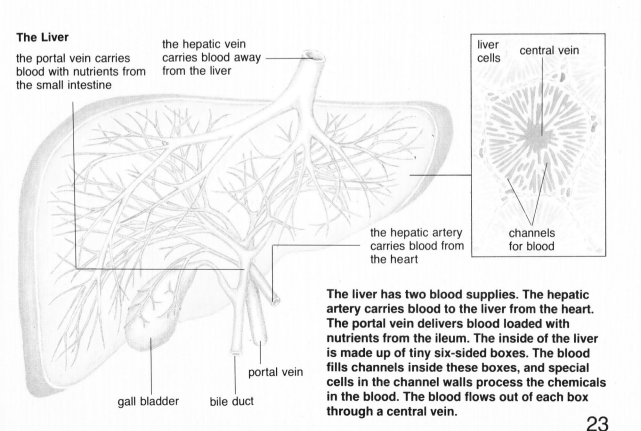

The Liver

the portal vein carries blood with nutrients from the small intestine

the hepatic vein carries blood away from the liver

the hepatic artery carries blood from the heart

liver cells

central vein

channels for blood

gall bladder

bile duct

portal vein

The liver has two blood supplies. The hepatic artery carries blood to the liver from the heart. The portal vein delivers blood loaded with nutrients from the ileum. The inside of the liver is made up of tiny six-sided boxes. The blood fills channels inside these boxes, and special cells in the channel walls process the chemicals in the blood. The blood flows out of each box through a central vein.

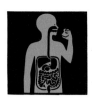

The Large Intestine

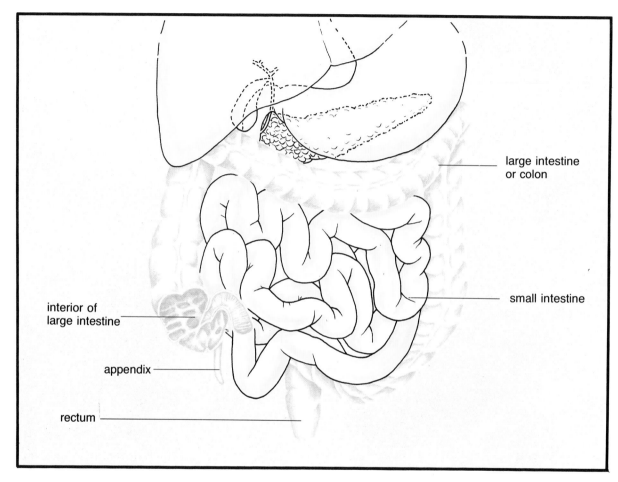

large intestine or colon

small intestine

interior of large intestine

appendix

rectum

The remains of the food after the digested nutrients have passed into the bloodstream pass from the ileum to the large intestine or **colon.** What is now left is waste, made up of dietary fiber mixed with water.

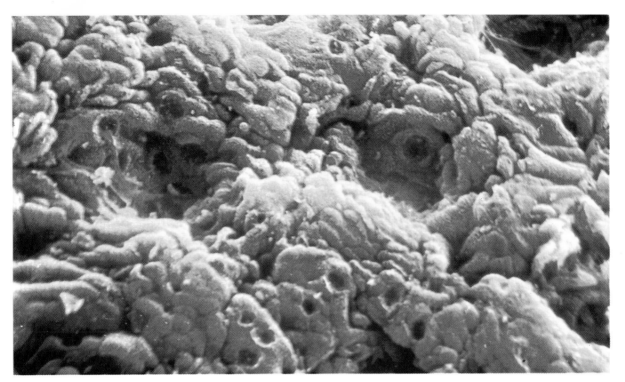

The photograph shows the muscles of the walls of the colon which squeeze the water out of the waste. The water goes out through the walls of the large intestine, and the muscles push the bulky waste along the colon to the rectum. The waste, which is now dry and solid, passes out through the rectum when you go to the toilet.

wash your hands well after going to the toilet

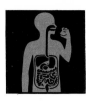

The Kidneys

We take water in when we eat, drink, and breathe, and we pass it out again when we sweat and go to the toilet. This athlete is drinking to replace the water he is losing by sweating.

about half our body weight is water

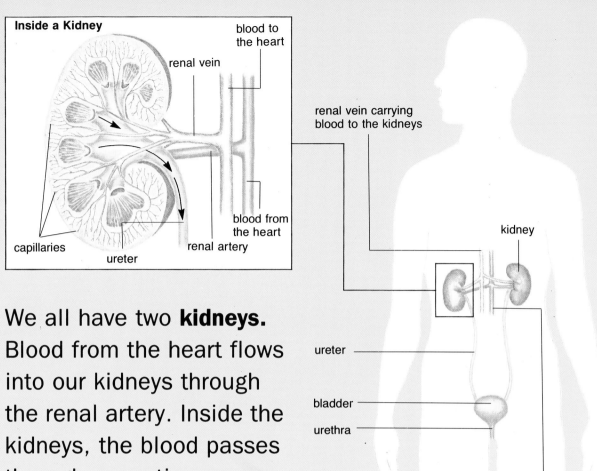

Inside a Kidney

blood to the heart

renal vein

renal vein carrying blood to the kidneys

blood from the heart

kidney

capillaries

renal artery

ureter

ureter

bladder

urethra

renal artery carrying blood from the heart

We all have two **kidneys.** Blood from the heart flows into our kidneys through the renal artery. Inside the kidneys, the blood passes through many tiny **capillaries.** Here the blood is filtered and poisons and waste water are taken out of it. The clean blood leaves the kidneys through the renal vein.

The waste water, called urine, flows from each kidney through a tube, the ureter, to the **bladder.**

As the bladder fills with urine it swells, and we feel the need to go to the toilet. The urine leaves the bladder through a tube called the urethra. We pass out about a quart of urine a day.

27

Input and Output

Oil and coal are fuels that provide the energy for machines to do things. The fuel that provides your body with energy is the food you eat.

Energy is measured in units called **calories.**

Different kinds of food contain different amounts of calories. If you eat food with more calories than your body needs, the extra food is stored as fat.

Input	calories	Output for one hour	calories
cup of cocoa, with milk and sugar	240	watching television	85
1 tsp sugar	25	reading	85
1 boiled egg	90	writing	115
cup of milk	100	cycling fast	600
2 slices bacon	300	soccer	650
3 slices bread	240	tennis	450
3.5 oz. chocolate	575	basketball	550
2 sausages	400	jogging	600
7 oz. steak	390	hiking	400

The table shows the amounts of calories in some different foods. You can also see how many calories the body uses up during one hour of exercise. Jogging, cycling, or hiking use up calories more quickly than when you are reading or watching television.

A Poor Diet

The picture shows sailors loading supplies onto ships 300 years ago.

Sailors used to eat limes. Limes contain vitamin C and stopped them from getting a disease called scurvy.

cells starved of oxygen

In many countries today many people suffer from **malnutrition.** The food they eat does not have the right amounts of nutrients for good health. A shortage of vitamin D, for example, can cause a disease called rickets. Children with rickets have soft bones and their legs may become misshapen.

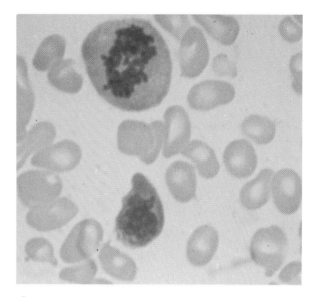

Our blood is made up of two kinds of blood cells. White blood cells help the body fight disease. Red blood cells carry **oxygen** from the air we breathe around the body. To do this, they need iron. If we do not take enough iron into our bodies, we may suffer from a disease called anemia.

The photograph shows some blood cells that have been starved of oxygen.

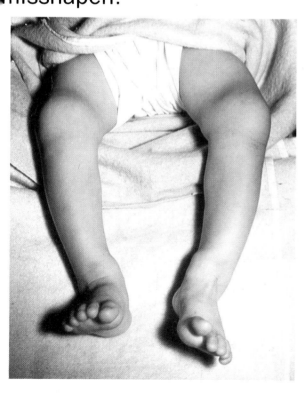

a baby with rickets

Not Enough Food

In some countries there is not enough rain for the farmers to grow any crops. People there may starve. They may have to rely on food sent from countries where the crops are good.

In these countries there is often far more food grown than can be eaten, so the extra food is stored or sold abroad.

extra wheat piled up in Nebraska

32

These Welsh children are going on a sponsored walk to raise money to help people in countries without enough food. Charities collect this money and send out emergency food supplies.

Charities also help set up long-term projects to help the farmers in countries with poor harvests so they can produce more food for themselves. A supply of water or tools for farming may be better gifts than food.

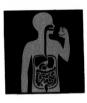

The Wrong Kinds of Food

The picture shows a flour mill, where wheat is ground into flour. Brown whole wheat flour is better for us than white flour because the husks of the grain add fiber to our diet.

meat fat is high in cholesterol

Our bodies need small amounts of fat but eating food like french fries and hamburgers may give us more fat than we need.

Animal products such as meat, eggs, and milk contain **cholesterol.** Too much cholesterol can build up in the blood and clog up the blood vessels around the heart. It causes heart disease. Oils made from sunflower seeds can reduce our levels of cholesterol.

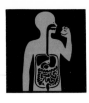

Eating for Health

A **balanced diet** contains a wide range of foods which provide carbohydrates, protein, and a small amount of fat. Vitamins and fiber also keep us healthy. How many different foods can you see in the picture?

If you eat too much candy, the sugar can cause bacteria to grow in your mouth. These bacteria attack your teeth and cause decay.

People who study diet and its effect on the body are called nutritionists. They help plan menus for patients in hospitals.

People's eating habits are formed when they are very young. If you are used to eating very sweet things and lots of fried food, it is not always easy to retrain your tastes. It is better to eat a balanced diet.

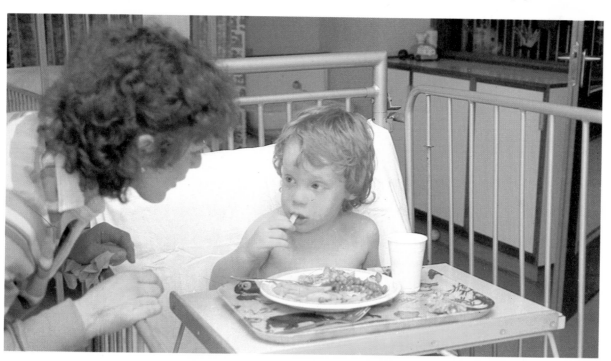

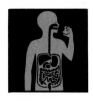

Food and Illness

The picture shows machines in a dairy. The milk inside the machines is being heated to kill the different bacteria in it. If we eat food with harmful bacteria, we may become ill and have to go to a hospital.

this poster warns Russians of the dangers of alcohol

Bacteria are easily spread from our bodies, from cuts and scratches, or from animals. Bacteria on our hands may be passed on to our food. Always wash your hands before touching food.

Keeping food cold in a refrigerator helps prevent bacteria from spreading.

ЗЛОУПОТРЕБЛЕНИЕ АЛКОГОЛЕМ

ТАК РАЗВИВАЮТСЯ

**ГАСТРИТЫ,
КОЛИТЫ,
ЯЗВЕННАЯ БОЛЕЗНЬ,
ЗАБОЛЕВАНИЯ ПЕЧЕНИ**

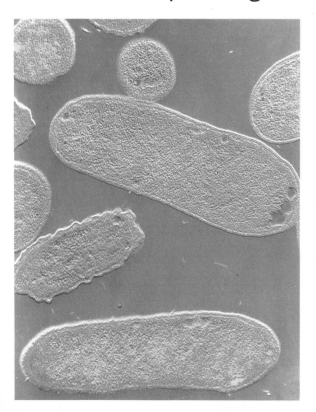

Salmonella bacteria are found in meat and poultry. Salmonella can cause sickness and diarrhea if they are eaten. However, they are killed if the food is well cooked.

Alcohol in large amounts is a poison and can damage a person's liver if they drink too much of it.

salmonella bacteria

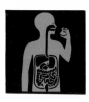

Medicine Today

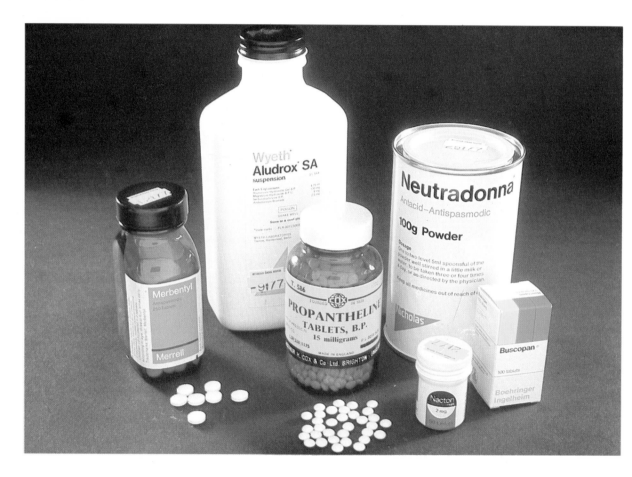

There are many different medicines to calm down an upset stomach. Some upsets may be mild and just make you feel slightly ill. More serious upsets need to be treated with drugs that kill bacteria without harming human cells.

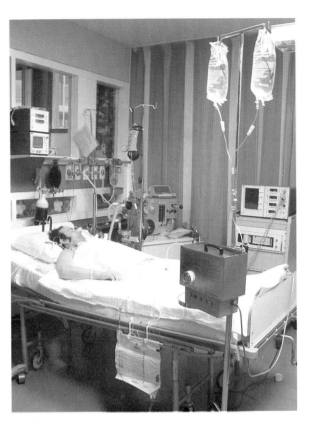

After some operations in the hospitals when people are very ill, they may not be able to digest their food properly. The nutrients that they need can be fed straight into the patient's bloodstream through an **intravenous drip** hooked up to a person's vein.

A kidney machine can take over the job of cleaning the blood if the kidneys are damaged or stop working properly.

this patient is on an intravenous drip

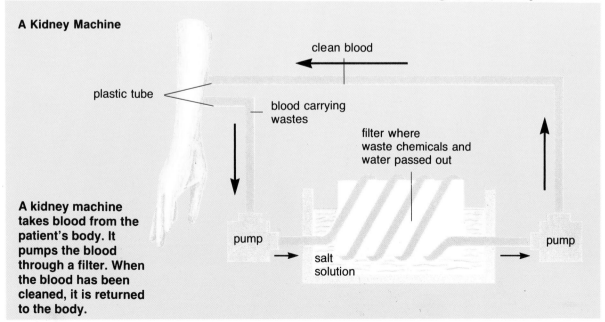

A Kidney Machine

clean blood

plastic tube

blood carrying wastes

filter where waste chemicals and water passed out

A kidney machine takes blood from the patient's body. It pumps the blood through a filter. When the blood has been cleaned, it is returned to the body.

pump

salt solution

pump

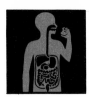

Public Health

Many diseases can be spread if food is prepared in dirty places. People who work in kitchens must keep themselves and everything they use very clean. Public health inspectors check restaurants and hotels regularly to make sure they are spotlessly clean.

Inspectors also make sure that only food of the right quality is for sale.

Public health also means that people make sure that **sewage** and other garbage is gotten rid of so that there is no danger to people's health.

bacteria live in dirty kitchens so everything must be kept clean

a sewage system cleans sewage and waste water from our houses

Food in the Future

In space there is no air and things have no weight.

This astronaut is doing an experiment to find out how plants would grow inside a spacecraft. In the future it may be possible to build huge spacecraft where crops can be grown and harvested by robots.

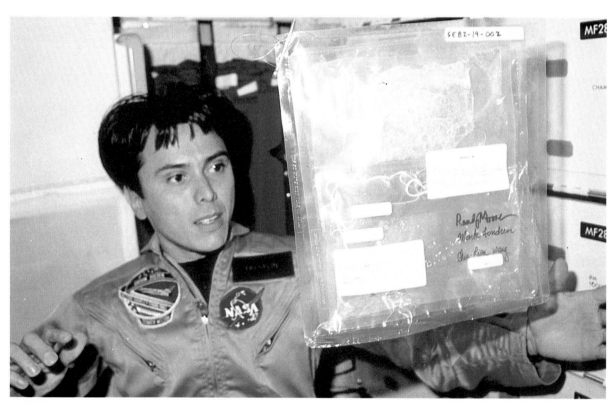

irrigating crops in Israel

Scientists are always looking for new ways to grow more food. **Irrigation** now makes it possible to grow crops in the dry desert.

In the future, farms may be built deep beneath the waves of the ocean. Fish and shellfish could be grown in large tanks.

Seaweed could be grown on the ocean floor.

a farm under the sea

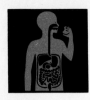

Glossary

bacteria   tiny creatures seen only by a strong microscope. Some bacteria are helpful, others cause diseases.

balanced diet   the right amounts and kinds of food for healthy living.

bile   a bitter, greenish liquid made in the liver which helps us digest fat.

bladder   the "bag" in which urine collects before it is passed out of the body.

blood vessels   tubes that carry blood around the body.

calories   a measure of the energy in food.

capillary   a very thin tube that carries blood in the body.

carbohydrate   an energy-giving substance.

cell   a very tiny part of living matter.

cholesterol   a fatty substance carried in the blood.

colon   another name for the large intestine.

dentine   the main yellow layer of a tooth beneath the hard outer surface.

dietary fiber   the hard, woody parts in fruit and vegetables.

duodenum   part of the small intestine after the stomach.

enamel   the very hard outer surface of a tooth.

energy   the power to do work.

enzymes   substances made by the body to speed up its reactions.

epiglottis   a "trapdoor" that prevents food blocking our trachea as we swallow.

esophagus   the tube leading from the throat to the stomach.

fat   an energy-giving substance found in some plant and all animal foods.

food chain   the way in which a large animal eats a smaller animal, and is then eaten by yet a larger animal.

gall bladder   part of the body that stores bile.

glucose   a simple sugar that the body uses as a fuel.

glycogen   the form in which glucose is stored in the blood.

heart   the part of the body that pumps the blood around it.

ileum   the part of the small intestine where digested food is absorbed into the body.

intravenous drip   a way of passing food and other

chemicals directly into someone's bloodstream using a tube and a needle.

irradiation using special rays to kill germs in food.

irrigation watering dry areas so that crops can grow.

kidneys bean-shaped organs in the body that get rid of our waste water by making urine.

large intestine the shorter, second part of the intestine.

liver the place in the body where parts of your food are made into glycogen and urea, a basis of urine.

lungs the two sponge-like parts of the body used for breathing.

malnutrition when someone does not get enough nutrients to stay healthy.

microscope an instrument that makes very tiny objects look a lot larger.

minerals chemicals such as iron and calcium that the body needs to stay healthy.

mucus a slimy substance made by some parts of the body as a protective layer.

muscle a type of tissue in the body that makes it move.

nerve fibers tiny "cables" that pass messages between parts of the body and the brain.

nutrients the parts of food that can be used for energy, health, or growth.

oxygen a gas found in air and water. We need it to breathe and to release the energy in our food.

pancreas part of the body that makes digestive juices.

proteins parts of food needed for growing and repairing all living things.

rectum the end part of the large intestine.

saliva a clear liquid made in the mouth that helps us digest starchy foods and swallow.

sewage a mixture of water and human waste.

small intestine the first and longest part of the intestine, where food is broken down.

soft palate a flap of skin that blocks off the opening to the nose when you swallow.

sphincter a ring of muscle.

trachea a tube from the mouth and nose to the lungs.

urine the waste water that passes out of the body.

villi tiny finger-like lumps in the small intestine that help to absorb digested food.

vitamins substances in foods that keep the body well.

Index

© Heinemann Children's Reference 1990
Artwork © BLA Publishing Limited 1987

Material used in this book first appeared in Macmillan World Library: *How Our Bodies Work: Food and Digestion.* Published by Heinemann Children's Reference.

Photographic credits
(t = top b = bottom l = left r = right)
cover: © James Minor
4 The Hutchison Library; 5 S. & R. Greenhill, 6t Michael Holford; 6 The Ancient Art and Architecture Collection; 7 Vivien Fifield; 8 Vision International; 9t Tesco Stores Ltd; 9b Trevor Hill; 10t S. & R. Greenhill; 10b ZEFA; 12 Vision International; 13t Biophoto Associates; 13b Frank Lane Picture Agency; 14t Bruce Coleman Limited; 14b Vision International; 16t S. & R. Greenhill; 16b Vision International; 21t, 21b Science Photo Library; 22 Sporting Pictures; 25t Science Photo Library; 25t Vision International; 26 Sporting Pictures; 28 Trevor Hill; 29 S. & R. Greenhill; 30 Vivien Fifield; 31t Biophoto Associates; 31b Vision International; 32t The Hutchison Library; 32b Colorific; 33 Oxfam; 34 RHM Centre; 35t Vision International; 35b S. & R. Greenhill; 36 Vision International; 37t S. & R. Greenhill; 37b Camilla Jessel; 38 National Dairy Council; 39t Vision International; 39b Science Photo Library; 40 Biophoto Associates; 41 ZEFA; 42 Trevor Hill; 43t S. & R. Greenhill; 43b Vision International; 44 Science Photo Library; 45 Eric & David Hoskings